Easy French Cookbook

50 Authentic French Recipes

By
Chef Maggie Chow
Copyright © 2015 by Saxonberg Associates
All rights reserved

Published by
BookSumo, a division of Saxonberg Associates
http://www.booksumo.com/

INTRODUCTION

Welcome to *The Effortless Chef Series*! Thank you for taking the time to download the *Easy French Cookbook*. Come take a journey with me into the delights of easy cooking. The point of this cookbook and all my cookbooks is to exemplify the effortless nature of cooking simply.

In this book we focus on French cuisine. You will find that even though the recipes are simple, the taste of the dishes is quite amazing.

So will you join me in an adventure of simple cooking? If the answer is yes (and I hope it is) please consult the table of contents to find the dishes you are most interested in. Once you are ready jump right in and start cooking.

— Chef Maggie Chow

Table of Contents

Introduction 2

Table of Contents 3

Any Issues? Contact Me 8

Legal Notes 9

Common Abbreviations 10

Chapter 1: Easy French Recipes 11

    Crème Brulee 11

    Cordon Pork 14

    French Dessert I (Madeleines) (Lemon Cookies) 16

    Onion Soup I 19

    Swiss and Bacon Quiche 21

    Burgundy Beef I 23

    French Potato Bake 25

    (Au Gratin) 25

Maggie's Easy Cordon Bleu 28

Maggie's Easy Crepes I 30

Restaurant Style Onion Soup 32

Classical French Style Bread 35

Parmesan, Eggplant, and Mushroom Bake (Ratatouille) 38

Salmon with Lemon Sauce 41

Parisian Stew 44

French Dump Dinner I 46

Tapenade I (French Spice with Figs and Rosemary) 48

(Toasted Bread Dip) 48

Gruyere (Buttery Chicken) 51

Tapenade II (Olives, Garlic, and Parsley) (Bread Dip) 54

Gruyere Pie 56

Artisan Mozzarella Bake of Garlic and Artichokes 58

Southern French Rice 60

Southern French Spice Mix 62

(Herbes de Provence) 62

French Style Dump Dinner II 65
(Cannellini and Kielbasa) 65
Restaurant Style Asparagus 67
Easy Filet Mignon 69
Homemade French Dressing 71
Classical Coq Au Vin 73
(Chicken and Wine with Shallots and Mushrooms) 73
Maggie's Easier Coq Au Vin 76
Lemon and Butter Chicken 78
French Dessert II 80
(Vanilla Puffs) 80
French Style Honey Mustard Chicken with Tarragon 83
French Appetizer 86
(Toasted French Bread with Nuts and Parsley) 86
Mango Brie 88
Shallot Soup 90
Country Side Pie of Seasoned Pork and Beef 92

Garlic Potato Bake 95

French Dessert III (Walnut Fruit Pie) 98

Mushroom Sauce 101

Creamy Chicken and Sherry 103

Burgundy Beef II 105

Buttery Egg Bites 108

Crepes II 110

(Vegan Approved) 110

Mushrooms and Angel Hair 112

Apple Tenderloins 115

Easy French Canadian Style Poutine 118

(Fries with Mozzarella and Gravy) 118

Mediterranean Salad 120

Quiche II (Chards and Onions) 122

French Bean Casserole 124

Salad II 126

(Olives, Potatoes, and Roma Tomatoes) 126

Quinoa XL (Creamy Casserole of Broccoli and Mushrooms) 128

THANKS FOR READING! NOW LET'S TRY SOME **SUSHI** AND **DUMP DINNERS**.... 131

Come On.. 133

Let's Be Friends :).. 133

Can I Ask A Favour?... 134

Interested in Other Easy Cookbooks? 135

ANY ISSUES? CONTACT ME

If you find that something important to you is missing from this book please contact me at maggie@booksumo.com.

I will try my best to re-publish a revised copy taking your feedback into consideration and let you know when the book has been revised with you in mind.

:)

— Chef Maggie Chow

LEGAL NOTES

ALL RIGHTS RESERVED. NO PART OF THIS BOOK MAY BE REPRODUCED OR TRANSMITTED IN ANY FORM OR BY ANY MEANS. PHOTOCOPYING, POSTING ONLINE, AND / OR DIGITAL COPYING IS STRICTLY PROHIBITED UNLESS WRITTEN PERMISSION IS GRANTED BY THE BOOK'S PUBLISHING COMPANY. LIMITED USE OF THE BOOK'S TEXT IS PERMITTED FOR USE IN REVIEWS WRITTEN FOR THE PUBLIC AND/OR PUBLIC DOMAIN.

Common Abbreviations

cup(s)	C.
tablespoon	tbsp
teaspoon	tsp
ounce	oz.
pound	lb

*All units used are standard American measurements

Chapter 1: Easy French Recipes

Crème Brulee

Ingredients

- 1/2 C. semi-sweet chocolate chips
- 2 C. heavy cream
- 1/4 C. white sugar
- 1 pinch salt
- 2 tsps vanilla extract
- 5 egg yolks
- 4 tbsps white sugar

Directions

- Get a big pot of water boiling and then set your oven to 300 degrees before doing anything else.
- Get 4 ramekin dishes and put two tbsps of chocolate pieces into each.
- For 40 secs melt the chocolate in the microwave then stir it.
- If the chocolate is not melted heat everything again and also stir the chocolate again.
- Heat the following until steam forms: salt, sugar (1/4 C.), and cream.
- Get a bowl, combine: vanilla and cream.
- Add a ladle full of the hot sugar mix to the bowl and continue stirring. Then add some more to get the eggs hot.

- Add everything to the ramekins equally.
- Layer a towel in a casserole dish and then place the ramekins on top, add in the boiling water to the halfway mark of the ramekins and then cover everything in foil.
- Cook the contents in the oven for 42 mins.
- Then place everything in the fridge for 8 hours.
- Add a garnishing of sugar (1 tbsp) to each, then place the dish under the broiler for 4 mins.
- Enjoy.

Amount per serving (4 total)

Timing Information:

Preparation	10 m
Cooking	40 m
Total Time	6 h 50 m

Nutritional Information:

Calories	680 kcal
Fat	55.8 g
Carbohydrates	42.6g
Protein	6.6 g
Cholesterol	419 mg
Sodium	1155 mg

* Percent Daily Values are based on a 2,000 calorie diet.

Cordon Pork

Ingredients

- 2 boneless pork loin chops, butterflied
- 4 oz. crumbled blue cheese
- 2 slices bacon - cooked and crumbled
- 2 tbsps chopped fresh chives
- garlic salt to taste
- ground black pepper to taste
- chopped fresh parsley for garnish

Directions

- Coat a casserole dish with oil or nonstick spray and then set your oven to 325 degrees before doing anything else.
- Get a bowl, mix: chives, bacon, and cheese.
- Form two balls from this mix with your hands.
- Add each ball, to the center of each piece of pork.
- Roll up the pork and stake a toothpick through it.
- Add a topping of pepper and garlic salt to each one before layering everything into your dish.
- Cook the pork in the oven for 25 mins until fully done.
- Top the rolls with some parsley.
- Enjoy.

Amount per serving (2 total)

Timing Information:

Preparation	15 m
Cooking	20 m
Total Time	35 m

Nutritional Information:

Calories	394 kcal
Fat	26.3 g
Carbohydrates	2g
Protein	36 g
Cholesterol	108 mg
Sodium	1131 mg

* Percent Daily Values are based on a 2,000 calorie diet.

French Dessert I (Madeleines) (Lemon Cookies)

Ingredients

- 2 eggs
- 1/2 tsp vanilla extract
- 1/2 tsp lemon zest
- 1 C. confectioners' sugar
- 3/4 C. all-purpose flour
- 1/4 tsp baking powder
- 1/2 C. butter, melted and cooled

Directions

- Coat a madeleine dish with nonstick spray and then set your oven to 375 degrees before doing anything else.
- Get a bowl, combine: lemon zest, eggs, and vanilla. Use a mixer and continue mixing for 6 mins.
- Begin to add in the confectioners' and mix the contents for 6 more mins until everything is thick.
- Get a 2nd bowl, combine: baking powder, and flour.
- Add a quarter of the of the baking powder mix to the eggs and stir it in.
- Continue in this manner until everything is combined evenly.
- Finally add the butter and mix the contents again.

- Fill your madeleine dish with the batter and cook it in the oven for 13 mins.
- Let the contents cool for 2 mins then remove the cookies and top them with more sugar.
- Enjoy.

Amount per serving (12 total)

Timing Information:

Preparation	10 m
Cooking	30 m
Total Time	50 m

Nutritional Information:

Calories	148 kcal
Fat	8.6 g
Carbohydrates	16.1g
Protein	1.9 g
Cholesterol	51 mg
Sodium	77 mg

* Percent Daily Values are based on a 2,000 calorie diet.

Onion Soup I

Ingredients

- 4 onions, chopped
- 3 tbsps butter
- 3 tbsps all-purpose flour
- 1 tsp ground black pepper
- 1 tsp white sugar
- 3 (10.5 oz.) cans beef broth
- 1 1/4 C. water
- 1/2 tsp dried parsley
- 1/4 tsp dried thyme
- 1 C. white wine
- 1 French baguette, cut into 1/2 inch slices
- 8 oz. shredded mozzarella cheese

Directions

- Stir fry your onions in butter for 12 mins then add in: sugar, flour, and black pepper.
- Cook and stir for 2 mins before adding in: thyme, broth, parsley, and water.
- Let this mix gently boil for 12 mins.
- At the same time turn on your broiler.
- Divide the mix between the serving bowls and add a piece of bread to each with a final topping of cheese.
- Melt the cheese under the broiler or in the oven then serve the soup.
- Enjoy.

Amount per serving (6 total)

Timing Information:

Preparation	10 m
Cooking	30 m
Total Time	50 m

Nutritional Information:

Calories	476 kcal
Fat	15.2 g
Carbohydrates	56.1g
Protein	21.8 g
Cholesterol	36 mg
Sodium	1224 mg

* Percent Daily Values are based on a 2,000 calorie diet.

Swiss and Bacon Quiche

Ingredients

- 1 recipe pastry for a 9 inch single crust pie
- 6 slices bacon
- 1 onion, sliced
- 3 eggs, beaten
- 1 1/2 C. milk
- 1/4 tsp salt
- 1 1/2 C. shredded Swiss cheese
- 1 tbsp all-purpose flour

Directions

- Place some foil around a pastry shell and then set your oven to 450 degrees before doing anything else. Cook the pastry for 9 mins in the oven then take off the foil and cook the contents for 4 more mins. Then place it on the counter. Lower the heat of the oven to 325 degrees before continuing. Now stir fry your bacon, break it into pieces, and place it to the side. Stir fry the onions in the drippings, until they are soft, and remove any excess oils.
- Get a bowl, combine: eggs, salt, milk, onions, and bacon.
- Get a 2nd bowl, combine: flour and cheese.
- Combine both bowls and then fill your pastry shell with the mix.
- Cook the quiche in the oven for 37 mins.
- Serve when then pie has cooled off considerably. Enjoy.

Amount per serving (8 total)

Timing Information:

Preparation	30 m
Cooking	35 m
Total Time	1 h 5 m

Nutritional Information:

Calories	359 kcal
Fat	26.3 g
Carbohydrates	17g
Protein	13.6 g
Cholesterol	106 mg
Sodium	463 mg

* Percent Daily Values are based on a 2,000 calorie diet.

Burgundy Beef I

Ingredients

- 1/4 C. all-purpose flour
- 1 tsp salt
- 1/2 tsp ground black pepper
- 2 lbs cubed stew meat
- 4 tbsps butter
- 1 onion, chopped
- 2 carrots, chopped
- 1 clove garlic, minced
- 2 C. red wine
- 1 bay leaf
- 3 tbsps chopped fresh parsley
- 1/2 tsp dried thyme
- 1 (6 oz.) can sliced mushrooms
- 1 (16 oz.) can canned onions

Directions

- Get a bowl, combine: pepper, salt, and flour.
- Add in the beef, and stir the contents. Sear the beef in butter, then place everything into a baking dish. Set your oven to 350 degrees before doing anything else. Now begin to stir fry your onions, garlic, and carrots for 7 mins. Add in: the mushroom liquid, wine, thyme, bay leaf, and parsley.
- Top the meat with this mix and cook everything in the oven for 2.5 hrs with a covering of foil. Take off the foil and add the mushrooms and canned onions.
- Cook the meat for 35 more mins. Enjoy.

Amount per serving (4 total)

Timing Information:

Preparation	20 m
Cooking	3 h
Total Time	3 h 20 m

Nutritional Information:

Calories	583 kcal
Fat	31 g
Carbohydrates	21.9g
Protein	32.2 g
Cholesterol	125 mg
Sodium	1333 mg

* Percent Daily Values are based on a 2,000 calorie diet.

French Potato Bake
(Au Gratin)

Ingredients

- 4 russet potatoes, sliced into 1/4 inch slices
- 1 onion, sliced into rings
- salt and pepper to taste
- 3 tbsps butter
- 3 tbsps all-purpose flour
- 1/2 tsp salt
- 2 C. milk
- 1 1/2 C. shredded Cheddar cheese

Directions

- Coat a baking dish with butter and then set your oven to 400 degrees before doing anything else.
- Add half of the potatoes to the dish and then layer the onions on top.
- Add the rest of the potatoes and top them with pepper and salt.
- Begin to heat and stir your butter with salt and flour for 2 mins then add the milk and continue stirring and heating until it has become thick.
- Add the cheese and continue stirring for 40 more secs until it is all melted.

- Top the baking dish contents with the melted cheese mix and place a covering of foil over the dish.
- Cook everything in the oven for 90 mins.
- Enjoy after cooling for 12 mins.

Amount per serving (4 total)

Timing Information:

Preparation	30 m
Cooking	1 h 30 m
Total Time	2 h

Nutritional Information:

Calories	499 kcal
Fat	25.4 g
Carbohydrates	49.3g
Protein	19.8 g
Cholesterol	77 mg
Sodium	683 mg

* Percent Daily Values are based on a 2,000 calorie diet.

Maggie's Easy Cordon Bleu

Ingredients

- 6 skinless, boneless chicken breast halves, flattened to 1/4 inch thickness
- 6 slices Swiss cheese
- 6 slices ham
- 3 tbsps all-purpose flour
- 1 tsp paprika
- 6 tbsps butter
- 1/2 C. dry white wine
- 1 tsp chicken bouillon granules
- 1 tbsp cornstarch
- 1 C. heavy whipping cream

Directions

- Get a bowl, combine: paprika and flour Layer a piece of ham and a piece of cheese on each piece of chicken then roll up the chicken and stake a toothpick through each one. Now dredge the rolls in the flour mix. Sear your chicken in hot butter then add in the bouillon and wine.
- Place a lid on the pot, set the heat to low, and let the contents cook for 35 mins.
- Now place the chicken to the side.
- Get a 2nd bowl, mix: cream and cornstarch.
- Add this to the pan which cooked the chicken and get it hot.
- Top the chicken with the sauce. Enjoy.

Amount per serving (6 total)

Timing Information:

Preparation	15 m
Cooking	45 m
Total Time	1 h

Nutritional Information:

Calories	584 kcal
Fat	40.9 g
Carbohydrates	7.7g
Protein	41.6 g
Cholesterol	195 mg
Sodium	655 mg

* Percent Daily Values are based on a 2,000 calorie diet.

Maggie's Easy Crepes I

Ingredients

- 1 C. all-purpose flour
- 2 eggs
- 1/2 C. milk
- 1/2 C. water
- 1/4 tsp salt
- 2 tbsps butter, melted

Directions

- Get a bowl, combine: butter, water, salt, eggs, milk, and flour.
- Mix this liquid until it is completely smooth and combined.
- Get your frying pan hot with oil before continuing.
- Fry a 1/4 C. of the mix in the frying pan for 2 mins then flip the crepe and fry for 2 more mins.
- Enjoy.

Amount per serving (4 total)

Timing Information:

Preparation	10 m
Cooking	20 m
Total Time	30 m

Nutritional Information:

Calories	216 kcal
Fat	9.2 g
Carbohydrates	25.5g
Protein	7.4 g
Cholesterol	111 mg
Sodium	235 mg

* Percent Daily Values are based on a 2,000 calorie diet.

Restaurant Style Onion Soup

Ingredients

- 4 tbsps butter
- 1 tsp salt
- 2 large red onions, thinly sliced
- 2 large sweet onions, thinly sliced
- 1 (48 fluid oz.) can chicken broth
- 1 (14 oz.) can beef broth
- 1/2 C. red wine
- 1 tbsp Worcestershire sauce
- 2 sprigs fresh parsley
- 1 sprig fresh thyme leaves
- 1 bay leaf
- 1 tbsp balsamic vinegar
- salt and freshly ground black pepper to taste
- 4 thick slices French or Italian bread
- 8 slices Gruyere or Swiss cheese slices, room temperature
- 1/2 C. shredded Asiago
- 4 pinches paprika

Directions

- Get some twine and tie together the following: bay leaf, thyme, and parsley.
- Top your red and sweet onions with salt and then fry them in butter for 37 mins.
- Try to stir the contents every 3 mins to avoid any burning.

- Add in: Worcestershire, beef and chicken broth, and red wine. Drop the tied spices in as well.
- Let this gently boil for 22 mins, with a low heat, and stir the mix at least 3 times. Take out the spices and add in some pepper, salt, and vinegar.
- Place a lid on the pot and let the contents continue to stay warm with a very low level of heat.
- Turn on the broiler and toast your bread under it for 2 mins then flip the pieces and toast for 2 more mins.
- Grab 4 bowls and add an equal amount of soup to each.
- Then add a piece of bread to each as well.
- Add a topping of 2 pieces of gruyere and an equal amount of asiago to the pieces of bread and some paprika.
- Cook the bowls under the broiler for 6 mins.
- Enjoy.

NOTE: As you broil, the cheese should melt over the sides and add a touch of elegance to your dish. This is intended!

Amount per serving (4 total)

Timing Information:

Preparation	15 m
Cooking	1 h
Total Time	1 h 15 m

Nutritional Information:

Calories	618 kcal
Fat	35.9 g
Carbohydrates	39.5g
Protein	29.7 g
Cholesterol	114 mg
Sodium	3433 mg

* Percent Daily Values are based on a 2,000 calorie diet.

Classical French Style Bread

Ingredients

- 6 C. all-purpose flour
- 2 1/2 (.25 oz.) packages active dry yeast
- 1 1/2 tsps salt
- 2 C. warm water (110 degrees F/45 degrees C)
- 1 tbsp cornmeal
- 1 egg white
- 1 tbsp water

Directions

- Get bowl, mix: salt, flour (2 C.), warm water (2 C.), and yeast.
- Use a mixer to combine the contents and then add in the rest of the flour, while continuing to stir.
- For 12 mins knead this dough then add it to a bowl that has been coated with oil.
- Place a covering over the bowl and let the dough rise until it has become twice its original size.
- Now break the dough into 2 pieces and let it sit for another 12 mins.
- Make sure you cover the dough again.

- Shape the dough pieces into two large rectangles.
- Place the doughs onto a baking sheet and top them with cornmeal and then brush them with 1 tbsp of water and some whisked egg whites.
- Set your oven to 375 degrees before doing anything else.
- Place of covering, again on the dough and let it sit for 37 mins.
- Divide the dough in 4 pieces and cook the pieces for 22 mins in the oven.
- Top the bread with more egg white and water.
- Continue cooking for 17 more mins.
- Let the bread cool before serving.
- Enjoy.

Amount per serving (30 total)

Timing Information:

Preparation	25 m
Cooking	40 m
Total Time	2 h 40 m

Nutritional Information:

Calories	94 kcal
Fat	0.3 g
Carbohydrates	19.5g
Protein	2.9 g
Cholesterol	0 mg
Sodium	119 mg

* Percent Daily Values are based on a 2,000 calorie diet.

Parmesan, Eggplant, and Mushroom Bake (Ratatouille)

Ingredients

- 2 tbsps olive oil
- 3 cloves garlic, minced
- 2 tsps dried parsley
- 1 eggplant, cut into 1/2 inch cubes
- salt to taste
- 1 C. grated Parmesan cheese
- 2 zucchini, sliced
- 1 large onion, sliced into rings
- 2 C. sliced fresh mushrooms
- 1 green bell pepper, sliced
- 2 large tomatoes, chopped

Directions

- Grease a baking dish with half of the olive oil and then set your oven to 350 degrees before doing anything else.
- Stir fry your garlic in the rest of the olive until seared then add in the eggplants and parsley.
- Continue stir frying for 12 more mins. Then add some pepper and salt.
- Layer the mix into your baking dish and top with parmesan.
- Layer the zucchini over the parmesan and then some salt and bit more parmesan.

- Now layer: tomatoes, onions, mushrooms, and bell peppers.
- Add any remaining ingredients then top the entire mix with more parmesan and some salt.
- Cook the dish for 50 mins in the oven.
- Enjoy.

Amount per serving (4 total)

Timing Information:

Preparation	15 m
Cooking	45 m
Total Time	1 h

Nutritional Information:

Calories	251 kcal
Fat	13.5 g
Carbohydrates	24.3g
Protein	12.7 g
Cholesterol	18 mg
Sodium	327 mg

* Percent Daily Values are based on a 2,000 calorie diet.

Salmon with Lemon Sauce

Ingredients

- 3 tbsps fresh lemon juice
- 1 tbsp olive oil
- Salt and pepper to taste
- 2 (6 oz.) skinless, boneless salmon fillets
- 3 egg yolks
- 1 tbsp hot water
- 1 C. butter, cut into small pieces
- 2 tbsps fresh lemon juice
- Salt and pepper to taste
- 2 tbsps chopped fresh chives

Directions

- Get a saucepan and add in: salmon, lemon juice, pepper, olive oil, salt, and water (add enough to just cover the salmon).
- Heat this mix until hot but not boiling.
- Cook the salmon like this until the temperature of the fish is 140 degrees or it is opaque in color.
- At the same time get some water boiling in a separate pan.
- Begin to beat your yolks in a bowl and once the water is boiling add some of it to the yolks and continue mixing for a few mins.
- Now place the bowl over the boiling water but it should not touching the water and continue whisking until the yolks have thickened.

- You do not want to scramble the yolks. You are creating a sauce (hollandaise).
- Now add a piece of butter and let it melt then add another until everything has been added to sauce.
- Place the bowl to the side and add: pepper, salt, and lemon juice.
- Top your cooked fish with the hollandaise and chives as well.
- Enjoy.

Amount per serving (2 total)

Timing Information:

Preparation	15 m
Cooking	10 m
Total Time	25 m

Nutritional Information:

Calories	1270 kcal
Fat	123.7 g
Carbohydrates	14.3g
Protein	38.6 g
Cholesterol	650 mg
Sodium	21153 mg

* Percent Daily Values are based on a 2,000 calorie diet.

Parisian Stew

Ingredients

- 1 1/2 lbs cubed beef stew meat
- 1/4 C. all-purpose flour
- 2 tbsps vegetable oil
- 2 (14.5 oz.) cans Italian-style diced tomatoes
- 1 (14 oz.) can beef broth
- 4 carrots, chopped
- 2 potatoes, peeled and chopped
- 3/4 tsp dried thyme
- 2 tbsps Dijon-style prepared mustard
- salt and pepper to taste

Directions

- Get a bowl, mix: flour and meat.
- Sear the meat in veggie oil then add some pepper and salt.
- Now add: thyme, tomatoes, potatoes, broth, and carrots.
- Get the mix boiling.
- Place a lid on the pot, set the heat to low, and gently boil the mix for 65 mins.
- Add in the mustard 10 mins before the simmering is finished, stir the mix, and continue cooking for the remaining time.
- Enjoy.

Amount per serving (8 total)

Timing Information:

Preparation	10 m
Cooking	1 h 20 m
Total Time	1 h 30 m

Nutritional Information:

Calories	343 kcal
Fat	20.1 g
Carbohydrates	20g
Protein	18.7 g
Cholesterol	57 mg
Sodium	491 mg

* Percent Daily Values are based on a 2,000 calorie diet.

French Dump Dinner I

Ingredients

- 6 skinless, boneless chicken breast halves
- 1 (10.75 oz.) can condensed cream of chicken soup
- 1 C. milk
- 4 oz. sliced ham
- 4 oz. sliced Swiss cheese
- 1 (8 oz.) package herbed dry bread stuffing mix
- 1/4 C. butter, melted

Directions

- Get a bowl, combine: milk and chicken soup. Add this to the crock pot as well as the chicken pieces on top of the soup.
- Add some Swiss and ham to each piece of meat and stir the contents a bit.
- Now add the stuffing and then some butter.
- Cook this on low for 5 hrs.
- Enjoy.

Amount per serving (6 total)

Timing Information:

Preparation	10 m
Cooking	3 h
Total Time	3 h 10 m

Nutritional Information:

Calories	484 kcal
Fat	21.1 g
Carbohydrates	35.4g
Protein	36.3 g
Cholesterol	112 mg
Sodium	1205 mg

* Percent Daily Values are based on a 2,000 calorie diet.

Tapenade I (French Spice with Figs and Rosemary)

(Toasted Bread Dip)

Ingredients

- 1 C. chopped dried figs
- 1/2 C. water
- 1 tbsp olive oil
- 2 tbsps balsamic vinegar
- 1 tsp dried rosemary
- 1 tsp dried thyme
- 1/4 tsp cayenne pepper
- 2/3 C. chopped kalamata olives
- 2 cloves garlic, minced
- salt and pepper to taste
- 1/3 C. chopped toasted walnuts (optional)
- 1 (8 oz.) package cream cheese

Directions

- Boil your water and figs until the fruits are soft.
- Once the liquid has mostly evaporated, shut the heat, and add in: pepper, cayenne, salt, olive oil, olives, thyme, garlic, balsamic, and rosemary.

- Place the mix in the fridge for 5 hrs with a covering.
- Top everything with cheese and nuts.
- Serve with bread.
- Enjoy.

Amount per serving (6 total)

Timing Information:

Preparation	15 m
Cooking	10 m
Total Time	4 h 25 m

Nutritional Information:

Calories	327 kcal
Fat	24 g
Carbohydrates	26.4g
Protein	5.2 g
Cholesterol	41 mg
Sodium	361 mg

* Percent Daily Values are based on a 2,000 calorie diet.

Gruyere (Buttery Chicken)

Ingredients

- 1/4 C. all-purpose flour
- 1/2 tsp salt
- 1/4 tsp pepper
- 1 tsp chopped fresh parsley
- 1/2 tsp dried dill weed
- 1/4 C. butter, divided
- 4 boneless, skinless chicken breast halves
- 1 lb fresh mushrooms
- 1 onion, sliced into rings
- 1/2 C. white wine
- 8 oz. Gruyere cheese, shredded

Directions

- Clean your pieces of chicken with fresh water and then set your oven to 350 degrees before doing anything else.
- Get a bowl, combine: dill, flour, parsley, salt, and pepper.
- Coat the chicken with this mix and then sear them in butter.

- Layer the chicken pieces in a casserole dish then continue to stir fry your onions and mushrooms, until brown, in more butter.
- Once the onions are brown, add in the wine, and let the contents boil for 4 mins.
- Top the chicken with this mushroom mix and cook everything in the oven for 25 mins with a covering of foil.
- Remove the foil and continue cooking for 15 more mins after adding the cheddar.
- Enjoy.

Amount per serving (4 total)

Timing Information:

Preparation	15 m
Cooking	30 m
Total Time	45 m

Nutritional Information:

Calories	557 kcal
Fat	33.2 g
Carbohydrates	13.5g
Protein	46.2 g
Cholesterol	160 mg
Sodium	630 mg

* Percent Daily Values are based on a 2,000 calorie diet.

Tapenade II (Olives, Garlic, and Parsley) (Bread Dip)

Ingredients

- 3 cloves garlic, peeled
- 1 C. pitted kalamata olives
- 2 tbsps capers
- 3 tbsps chopped fresh parsley
- 2 tbsps lemon juice
- 2 tbsps olive oil
- salt and pepper to taste

Directions

- Puree the following with a blender: olive oil, garlic, lemon juice, olives, parsley, and capers.
- Add in some pepper and salt.
- Enjoy with toasted bread.

Amount per serving (8 total)

Timing Information:

Preparation	15 m
Cooking	15 m
Total Time	15 m

Nutritional Information:

Calories	81 kcal
Fat	7.9 g
Carbohydrates	2.5g
Protein	0.5 g
Cholesterol	0 mg
Sodium	359 mg

* Percent Daily Values are based on a 2,000 calorie diet.

Gruyere Pie

Ingredients

- 1 (9 inch) refrigerated pie crust
- 2 tsps butter
- 3 leeks, chopped
- 1 pinch salt and black pepper to taste
- 1 C. light cream
- 1 1/4 C. shredded Gruyere cheese

Directions

- Set your oven to 375 degrees before doing anything else.
- Stir fry the leeks in butter for 12 mins then add some pepper and salt.
- Cook the mix for 1 more min before setting the heat to low and adding the cheese and cream.
- Get this mix hot and then add everything to the pie crust.
- Cook the pie, for 32 mins in the oven, then let it cool for 15 mins.
- Enjoy.

Amount per serving (6 total)

Timing Information:

Preparation	10 m
Cooking	40 m
Total Time	1 h

Nutritional Information:

Calories	365 kcal
Fat	26.8 g
Carbohydrates	20.7g
Protein	11.2 g
Cholesterol	57 mg
Sodium	300 mg

* Percent Daily Values are based on a 2,000 calorie diet.

Artisan Mozzarella Bake of Garlic and Artichokes

Ingredients

- 1 tbsp olive oil
- 1 clove garlic, minced
- 2 (6 oz.) cans artichoke hearts, drained
- 1/2 C. Italian seasoned bread crumbs
- 1/2 C. grated Parmesan cheese, divided
- 1 (9 inch) unbaked 9 inch pie crust
- 3 eggs, beaten
- 1 (8 oz.) package mozzarella cheese, shredded

Directions

- Set your oven to 350 degrees before doing anything else.
- Stir fry your garlic, until seared, then add in the artichokes, and fry the mix for 12 more mins. Now add the parmesan and the bread crumbs.
- Get everything hot and fill the pie shell with it.
- Top the pie with the beaten eggs and more parmesan.
- Now add the mozzarella.
- Cook the pie for 50 mins in the oven.
- Enjoy.

Amount per serving (7 total)

Timing Information:

Preparation	10 m
Cooking	45 m
Total Time	55 m

Nutritional Information:

Calories	365 kcal
Fat	22.7 g
Carbohydrates	24.1g
Protein	17.7 g
Cholesterol	106 mg
Sodium	774 mg

* Percent Daily Values are based on a 2,000 calorie diet.

Southern French Rice

Ingredients

- 1 C. white rice
- 2 C. chicken stock
- 1 1/2 tsps herbes de Provence
- 1 pinch sea salt
- 1 pinch pepper

Directions

- Get the following boiling: pepper, rice, salt, stock, and herbes.
- Once the rice is boiling, place a lid on the pot, set the heat to its lowest level, and cook for 22 mins.
- Once the rice has cooled stir it.
- Enjoy.

NOTE: See next recipe to make the spice mix.

Amount per serving (4 total)

Timing Information:

Preparation	2 m
Cooking	23 m
Total Time	25 m

Nutritional Information:

Calories	169 kcal
Fat	0.3 g
Carbohydrates	37.1g
Protein	3.3 g
Cholesterol	0 mg
Sodium	82 mg

* Percent Daily Values are based on a 2,000 calorie diet.

Southern French Spice Mix
(Herbes de Provence)

Ingredients

- 2 tbsps dried rosemary
- 1 tbsp fennel seed
- 2 tbsps dried savory
- 2 tbsps dried thyme
- 2 tbsps dried basil
- 2 tbsps dried marjoram
- 2 tbsps dried lavender flowers
- 2 tbsps dried Italian parsley
- 1 tbsp dried oregano
- 1 tbsp dried tarragon
- 1 tsp bay powder

Directions

- With a mortar and pestle, combine the following: fennel seeds, bay powder, rosemary, tarragon, savory, oregano, basil, parsley, lavender, and marjoram.
- Place the mix in a mason jar with a tight seal and store in the cupboard for continued use.
- Enjoy.

NOTE: This spice mix is native to the coast of Southern France. It is best used for veggies but can be enjoyed with baked meats as well. Use this mix in all recipes which call for *Herbes de Provence*.

Amount per serving (100 total)

Timing Information:

Preparation	
Cooking	5 m
Total Time	5 m

Nutritional Information:

Calories	2 kcal
Fat	0 g
Carbohydrates	0.3g
Protein	0.1 g
Cholesterol	0 mg
Sodium	< 1 mg

* Percent Daily Values are based on a 2,000 calorie diet.

French Style Dump Dinner II
(Cannellini and Kielbasa)

Ingredients

- 2 lbs skinless, boneless chicken breast halves, cut into chunks
- 1 onion, quartered and thinly sliced
- 2 large cloves garlic, minced
- 1/4 C. chopped fresh parsley
- 1/2 tsp salt
- 1/4 tsp black pepper
- 2 (15 oz.) cans cannellini beans, drained and rinsed
- 1 lb turkey kielbasa, cut into 1/2-inch slices
- 1/3 C. dry white wine

Directions

- Get a bowl, combine: kielbasa, onions, cannellini, parsley, pepper, and salt.
- Layer your chicken pieces first into the crock pot. Then top with the onion mix.
- Add in the wine and cook for 6 hrs with low heat.
- Enjoy.

Amount per serving (6 total)

Timing Information:

Preparation	20 m
Cooking	5 h
Total Time	5 h 20 m

Nutritional Information:

Calories	417 kcal
Fat	9.1 g
Carbohydrates	24.9g
Protein	51.4 g
Cholesterol	1135 mg
Sodium	1253 mg

* Percent Daily Values are based on a 2,000 calorie diet.

Restaurant Style Asparagus

Ingredients

- 1 bunch fresh asparagus spears, trimmed
- 2 tbsps olive oil
- 1 tbsp dried Herbes de Provence
- sea salt and pepper to taste

Directions

- Cover a casserole dish with foil and then set your oven to 400 degrees before doing anything else.
- Get a bowl, combine: pepper, asparagus, salt, olive oil, and Herbes de Provence.
- Place the veggies into the casserole dish and cook them in the oven for 15 mins.
- Enjoy.

Amount per serving (4 total)

Timing Information:

Preparation	5 m
Cooking	12 m
Total Time	17 m

Nutritional Information:

Calories	82 kcal
Fat	6.9 g
Carbohydrates	4.4g
Protein	2.5 g
Cholesterol	0 mg
Sodium	82 mg

* Percent Daily Values are based on a 2,000 calorie diet.

Easy Filet Mignon

Ingredients

- 1/4 C. coarsely crushed black peppercorns
- 4 (6 oz.) beef tenderloin filets, 1 1/2 inches thick
- salt to taste
- 1 tbsp butter
- 1 tsp olive oil
- 1/3 C. beef broth
- 1 C. heavy cream

Directions

- Coat the tenderloins with peppercorns and salt.
- For 4 mins, per side, cook your steaks, in butter and olive oil.
- Check the temperature of the meat for a 130 degree readout.
- Then wrap the meat with some foil.
- Add in the broth to same pan and scrape up the bottom bits.
- Now add in the cream and cook the contents for 8 mins with a low heat until it becomes sauce like.
- Add the tenderloins to the cream and cook for 2 more mins while flipping the meat in the sauce.
- Serve the steaks with a liberal topping of sauce.
- Enjoy.

Amount per serving (4 total)

Timing Information:

Preparation	10 m
Cooking	15 m
Total Time	25 m

Nutritional Information:

Calories	549 kcal
Fat	46.7 g
Carbohydrates	4.9g
Protein	27.5 g
Cholesterol	176 mg
Sodium	267 mg

* Percent Daily Values are based on a 2,000 calorie diet.

Homemade French Dressing

Ingredients

- 2/3 C. ketchup
- 3/4 C. white sugar
- 1/2 C. white wine vinegar
- 1/2 C. vegetable oil
- 1 small onion, quartered
- 2 tsps paprika
- 2 tsps Worcestershire sauce

Directions

- Puree the following: Worcestershire, ketchup, paprika, sugar, onions, vinegar, and oil.
- Once the mix is the consistency of a dressing place the contents into a mason jar with a tight seal.
- Place the dressing in the fridge and enjoy over salad.
- Enjoy.

Amount per serving (24 total)

Timing Information:

Preparation	5 m
Cooking	25 m
Total Time	5 m

Nutritional Information:

Calories	73 kcal
Fat	4.6 g
Carbohydrates	8.4g
Protein	0.2 g
Cholesterol	0 mg
Sodium	80 mg

* Percent Daily Values are based on a 2,000 calorie diet.

Classical Coq Au Vin

(Chicken and Wine with Shallots and Mushrooms)

Ingredients

- 6 bone-in, skin-on chicken thighs
- 1 pinch kosher salt and freshly ground black pepper to taste
- 8 oz. bacon, sliced crosswise into 1/2-inch pieces
- 10 large button mushrooms, quartered
- 1/2 large yellow onion, diced
- 2 shallots, sliced
- 2 tsps all-purpose flour
- 2 tsps butter
- 1 1/2 C. red wine
- 6 sprigs fresh thyme
- 1 C. chicken broth

Directions

- Set your oven to 375 degrees before doing anything else.
- Top the chicken with some pepper and salt and begin to fry your bacon for 12 mins.
- Now place the pieces to the side.

- With a high heat, sear the chicken in the drippings for 5 mins per side.
- Now remove them from the pan.
- Stir fry your onions, shallots, and mushrooms in the drippings as well over a lower level of heat for 10 mins, then add some salt.
- Add some butter and flour to the onions and cook the mix for 2 mins while stirring.
- Add in the wine and get everything boiling while scraping the bottom of the pan.
- Now add the thyme and bacon back to the boiling wine and cook the mix for 4 mins.
- Pour in the chicken broth and place the chicken thighs into the mix in as well.
- Get the mix gently boiling and then shut the heat.
- Place the pan in the oven for 35 mins.
- Now baste the chicken and cook for 30 more mins.
- Remove the chicken from the pan and place to the side for serving.
- Begin to heat the juices in the pan over a high heat on the stove for 6 mins and remove any fat from the sauce as it simmers.
- Add some pepper and salt and remove the thyme.
- Top the chicken liberally with the thick sauce.
- Enjoy.

Amount per serving (6 total)

Timing Information:

Preparation	15 m
Cooking	1 h 30 m
Total Time	1 h 45 m

Nutritional Information:

Calories	337 kcal
Fat	18 g
Carbohydrates	7.9g
Protein	24.4 g
Cholesterol	82 mg
Sodium	582 mg

* Percent Daily Values are based on a 2,000 calorie diet.

Maggie's Easier Coq Au Vin

Ingredients

- 1 tbsp vegetable oil
- 1 (4 lb) whole chicken, cut into pieces
- 1 tsp salt
- 1/4 tsp ground black pepper
- 1/4 tsp garlic powder
- 1 1/2 C. red wine
- 1 1/2 C. chicken stock
- 1 onion
- 1 tbsp cornstarch
- 1/3 C. water

Directions

- Top your chicken pieces with garlic powder, pepper, and salt.
- Sear them in oil for 6 mins.
- Now dip your pieces of chicken in the wine then place them back into the pan.
- Add the following to the chicken: onions, and the rest of the wine.
- Place a lid on the pan and cook the mix with a lower level of heat for 35 mins.
- Get a 2nd bowl, and combine: cornstarch and water.
- Cook this mix for 4 mins.
- Now combine the cornstarch mix with the wine mix and stir.
- Enjoy.

Amount per serving (8 total)

Timing Information:

Preparation	10 m
Cooking	35 m
Total Time	45 m

Nutritional Information:

Calories	344 kcal
Fat	17.9 g
Carbohydrates	3.7g
Protein	31.8 g
Cholesterol	100 mg
Sodium	498 mg

* Percent Daily Values are based on a 2,000 calorie diet.

Lemon and Butter Chicken

Ingredients

- 1/4 C. all-purpose flour, or as needed
- salt and black pepper to taste
- 2 eggs, beaten
- 1 tbsp white sugar
- 1 tbsp grated Parmesan cheese
- 2 tbsps olive oil
- 4 skinless, boneless chicken breast halves
- 1/4 C. butter
- 2 tsps minced garlic
- 1/4 C. dry sherry
- 1/4 C. lemon juice
- 2 tsps low-sodium chicken base

Directions

- Get a bowl, combine: pepper, flour, and salt.
- Get a 2nd bowl, add: parmesan, whisked eggs, and sugar.
- Coat your chicken with the flour mix first and then the parmesan mix.
- For 7 mins per side, cook the chicken in olive oil until fully done.
- Then place the pieces to the side. Now gently simmer your chicken base, lemon juice, sherry, and garlic, in the same pan, in melted butter.
- Cook this mix for 7 mins.
- Add the chicken back to the pan and cook everything for 17 more mins.
- Liberally top the chicken with the sauce. Enjoy.

Amount per serving (4 total)

Timing Information:

Preparation	15 m
Cooking	15 m
Total Time	30 m

Nutritional Information:

Calories	405 kcal
Fat	22.8 g
Carbohydrates	15g
Protein	32.7 g
Cholesterol	194 mg
Sodium	416 mg

* Percent Daily Values are based on a 2,000 calorie diet.

French Dessert II

(Vanilla Puffs)

Ingredients

- 1/2 C. white sugar
- 5 tbsps all-purpose flour
- 1 pinch salt
- 2 C. milk
- 2 egg yolks, beaten
- 1 tsp vanilla extract
- 1/2 C. shortening
- 1 C. water
- 1 C. all-purpose flour
- 1 pinch salt
- 4 eggs

Directions

- Get a bowl and whisk your yolks in it for 2 mins.
- Begin heating the following in a pan: salt, half C. sugar, and flour.
- While stirring, add in the milk gradually, and continue stirring.
- Once all the milk has been added get the contents boiling for 1 min.
- Now add some of this mix to your yolks and mix for 20 more secs.
- Add all the yolks to the pan and stir everything until smooth.
- Once the mix starts to boil add vanilla and shut the heat.

- Let the contents cool a bit then place a covering on the pan and place everything in the fridge until chilled.
- This is your custard filling.
- Now set your oven to 450 degrees before doing anything else.
- Get another pan and mix water and shortening.
- Get this mix boiling then add salt and 1 C. of flour.
- Combine this mix until a ball is formed.
- Shut the heat and one by one add your eggs while continue to stir.
- Now add tablespoons of this mix to a cookie sheet and then cook everything, for 12 mins, in the oven.
- After 12 mins of cooking lower the oven's temperature to 400 degrees and cook for 23 more mins.
- Let the pastries cool and then fill them with the custard mix.
- Enjoy.

Amount per serving (10 total)

Timing Information:

Preparation	15 m
Cooking	1 h
Total Time	1 h 30 m

Nutritional Information:

Calories	255 kcal
Fat	14.4 g
Carbohydrates	25.1g
Protein	6.4 g
Cholesterol	120 mg
Sodium	81 mg

* Percent Daily Values are based on a 2,000 calorie diet.

French Style Honey Mustard Chicken with Tarragon

Ingredients

- 3 tbsps Dijon mustard
- 2 tbsps honey
- 2 tbsps dried tarragon
- 2 tsps dried basil
- 2 tsps dried thyme
- 1/8 tsp salt
- 1/8 tsp freshly ground black pepper
- 2 tbsps vegetable oil
- 4 boneless, skinless chicken breast halves
- 1 C. white wine

Directions

- Get a bowl, combine: pepper, honey tarragon, thyme, salt, basil, and Dijon.
- Begin to fry your chicken in oil and top each piece with the honey mix.
- Once both sides are coated, add in a quarter of a C. of wine to the pan.
- Place a lid on the pan, and let chicken gently cook, over low heat, for 12 mins.
- At this point all liquid should be evaporated.
- Add in another quarter of a C. of wine and cook for 7 more mins.
- At this point the chicken should be fully done.

- Place it to the side.
- Add in the rest of the wine to the pan and turn up the heat.
- Stir and scrape the bottom of pan and let 1/3 of liquid evaporate with a light boil.
- Top the chicken with this sauce.
- Enjoy.

Amount per serving (4 total)

Timing Information:

Preparation	10 m
Cooking	25 m
Total Time	35 m

Nutritional Information:

Calories	298 kcal
Fat	8.5 g
Carbohydrates	14.8g
Protein	28.1 g
Cholesterol	68 mg
Sodium	437 mg

* Percent Daily Values are based on a 2,000 calorie diet.

French Appetizer

(Toasted French Bread with Nuts and Parsley)

Ingredients

- 1 French baguette, cut into 1/3 inch thick slices
- 1/4 C. butter, melted
- 4 oz. crumbled blue cheese
- 1/4 C. butter, softened
- salt and pepper to taste
- 1/2 C. chopped walnuts
- 1/2 C. chopped fresh parsley

Directions

- Melt your butter and then set your oven to 400 degrees before doing anything else.
- Coat one side of each of your pieces of bread with the butter and then layer the bread in a casserole dish with this side facing down.
- Get a bowl, combine: pepper, blue cheese, salt, and more butter.
- Top your bread with an even amount of this mix and then some nuts.
- Cook the bread in the oven for 7 mins then top the bread with some parsley.
- Enjoy.

Amount per serving (20 total)

Timing Information:

Preparation	10 m
Cooking	30 m
Total Time	40 m

Nutritional Information:

Calories	143 kcal
Fat	8.3 g
Carbohydrates	13.4g
Protein	4.4 g
Cholesterol	16 mg
Sodium	280 mg

* Percent Daily Values are based on a 2,000 calorie diet.

Mango Brie

Ingredients

- 1 (2.2 lb) wheel Brie cheese
- 2 tsps ground curry powder
- 1 (12 oz.) jar mango chutney
- 1 C. chopped cashews
- 1 French baguette, cut into 1/2 inch slices

Directions

- Set your oven to 350 degrees before doing anything else.
- Top your brie with the curry and press it in.
- Now top the coated brie with the chutney and then the nuts.
- Cook the brie in the oven, in a baking dish, for 17 mins, and serve it with some French bread.
- Enjoy.

Amount per serving (32 total)

Timing Information:

Preparation	10 m
Cooking	15 m
Total Time	25 m

Nutritional Information:

Calories	187 kcal
Fat	11 g
Carbohydrates	13.8g
Protein	9 g
Cholesterol	31 mg
Sodium	318 mg

* Percent Daily Values are based on a 2,000 calorie diet.

SHALLOT SOUP

Ingredients

- 2 tbsps butter
- 2 medium shallots, finely chopped
- 2 C. water
- 3 C. fresh shelled green peas
- salt and pepper to taste
- 3 tbsps whipping cream (optional)

Directions

- Stir fry your shallots in butter for 4 mins then add in: pepper, peas, salt, and water.
- Get everything boiling.
- Once the mix is boiling, place a lid on the pot, set the heat to low, and let the mix cook for 15 mins.
- Now puree the peas and add them to the pan along with the cream.
- Heat everything back up and then add more pepper and salt.
- Enjoy.

Amount per serving (4 total)

Timing Information:

Preparation	5 m
Cooking	12 m
Total Time	17 m

Nutritional Information:

Calories	195 kcal
Fat	10.3 g
Carbohydrates	20.2g
Protein	6.8 g
Cholesterol	31 mg
Sodium	202 mg

* Percent Daily Values are based on a 2,000 calorie diet.

COUNTRY SIDE PIE OF SEASONED PORK AND BEEF

Ingredients

- 1/2 lb lean ground beef
- 1/2 lb ground pork
- 1 small onion, finely chopped
- 1 clove garlic, minced
- 3/4 C. water
- 1 stalk celery, finely chopped
- 1 carrot, finely chopped
- 3 cubes chicken bouillon
- 1 bay leaf
- 1 baking potato, finely chopped
- 1/4 tsp ground black pepper
- 1/4 tsp ground cinnamon
- 1/8 tsp ground cloves
- 1/8 tsp ground nutmeg
- 1 (9 inch) unbaked deep dish pie crust
- 1 egg yolk
- 1 tbsp water

Directions

- Stir fry the following until browned: garlic, onions, and pork.
- Add: bay leaf, 3/4 C. of water, bouillon, celery, and carrots.
- Let this mix gently boil for 12 mins.
- Now set your oven to 350 degrees before doing anything else.

- Add the following to the carrot mix: nutmeg, potato, cloves, pepper, and cinnamon.
- Cook everything for 2 mins.
- Now shut the heat.
- Get a bowl, combine: 1 tbsp of water and egg yolk.
- Now coat your pie shell with this mix.
- Pour the carrot mix into the shell and add the top crust.
- Crimp the edges and cut some incisions into the top of the pie.
- Top the pie with more egg mix and cook everything in the oven for 50 mins.
- Enjoy.

Amount per serving (6 total)

Timing Information:

Preparation	30 m
Cooking	45 m
Total Time	1 h 15 m

Nutritional Information:

Calories	361 kcal
Fat	21.5 g
Carbohydrates	24.4g
Protein	16.7 g
Cholesterol	81 mg
Sodium	887 mg

* Percent Daily Values are based on a 2,000 calorie diet.

Garlic Potato Bake

Ingredients

- 2 lbs russet potatoes, skin removed, cut into 1/2 inch pieces
- 2 tbsps olive oil
- 4 onions, thinly sliced
- 2 tbsps chopped garlic
- 1/2 C. butter
- salt to taste
- ground white pepper, to taste
- 1 tbsp finely minced fresh parsley

Directions

- Set your oven to 400 degrees before doing anything else.
- Now boil your potatoes, in water, for 3 mins, then remove all the liquids.
- Begin to stir fry your onions, in olive oil, for 9 mins, and then add the garlic.
- Fry the garlic until it is tender and place this mix in a bowl.
- Place 1/3 of the potatoes into a frying pan over melted butter and add some pepper and salt.
- Add half of the onion mix, then 1/3 more of the potatoes.
- Add the remaining onion mix and then the last of the potatoes.
- Top everything with some pepper and salt.

- Cook the layers in the oven for 14 mins.
- Garnish the dish with parsley and serve.
- Enjoy.

Amount per serving (6 total)

Timing Information:

Preparation	30 m
Cooking	25 m
Total Time	55 m

Nutritional Information:

Calories	325 kcal
Fat	20.1 g
Carbohydrates	34.6g
Protein	3.5 g
Cholesterol	41 mg
Sodium	119 mg

* Percent Daily Values are based on a 2,000 calorie diet.

French Dessert III (Walnut Fruit Pie)

Ingredients

- 1/4 C. butter, softened
- 1 C. white sugar
- 1 egg
- 1/4 tsp salt
- 1 tsp ground cinnamon
- 1 tsp ground nutmeg
- 1 tsp baking soda
- 1 C. all-purpose flour
- 1/2 C. chopped walnuts
- 2 1/2 C. diced apple without peel
- 1 tsp vanilla extract
- 2 tbsps hot water
- 3 oz. cream cheese, softened
- 3 tbsps unsalted butter, softened
- 1/2 tsp vanilla extract
- 1 1/2 C. sifted confectioners' sugar

Directions

- Coat a pie pan with oil or nonstick spray and then set your oven to 350 degrees before doing anything else.
- Get a bowl, mix: hot water, 1/4 C. of butter, 1 tsp vanilla, sugar, apples, egg, nuts, salt, flour, cinnamon, soda, and nutmeg.
- Form a thick mix and then fill your pie pan with it.
- Cook everything in the oven for 50 mins.

- At the same time get a bowl, and mix: confectioners', cream cheese, 1/2 tsp vanilla, and 3 tbsps butter.
- Let the mix sit until the pie is done then spread the frosting before serving.
- Enjoy.

Amount per serving (8 total)

Timing Information:

Preparation	10 m
Cooking	1 h
Total Time	1 h 10 m

Nutritional Information:

Calories	453 kcal
Fat	19.6 g
Carbohydrates	67.6g
Protein	4.6 g
Cholesterol	62 mg
Sodium	313 mg

* Percent Daily Values are based on a 2,000 calorie diet.

Mushroom Sauce

Ingredients

- 1 tbsp butter
- 2 tbsps shallot, minced
- 1 tsp minced garlic (optional)
- 3 tbsps butter
- 2 C. sliced fresh mushrooms
- 1 C. beef broth
- 1/3 C. red wine
- 1 tbsp Worcestershire sauce
- 1 bay leaf
- 1/4 tsp chopped fresh thyme, or to taste
- salt and pepper to taste
- 1 tbsp cornstarch
- 2 tbsps cold water

Directions

- Stir fry your shallots and garlic in butter (1 tbsp), for 5 mins, then add the rest of the butter, and fry your mushrooms in it for 7 mins.
- Add in: thyme, broth, bay leaf, Worcestershire, and wine.
- Get the mix boiling for 1 min then set the heat to low and gently cook the contents for 35 mins.
- Now add in some pepper and salt.
- Combine some water and cornstarch and mix this into the mushroom mix and get everything hot.
- Enjoy.

Amount per serving (4 total)

Timing Information:

Preparation	25 m
Cooking	45 m
Total Time	1 h 10 m

Nutritional Information:

Calories	146 kcal
Fat	11.8 g
Carbohydrates	5.5g
Protein	2.1 g
Cholesterol	31 mg
Sodium	324 mg

* Percent Daily Values are based on a 2,000 calorie diet.

CREAMY CHICKEN AND SHERRY

Ingredients

- 6 bone-in chicken breast halves, with skin
- 1 (10.75 oz.) can condensed cream of mushroom soup
- 1 (4.5 oz.) can mushrooms, with liquid
- 1 C. sour cream
- 1/2 C. cooking sherry
- 1 tbsp paprika

Directions

- Set your oven to 350 degrees before doing anything else.
- Layer your chicken breasts with their skin facing upwards in a casserole dish.
- Get a bowl, mix: sherry, soup, sour cream, and mushrooms (with juice).
- Top the chicken with the sour cream mix and then add some paprika.
- Cook the chicken for 80 mins in the oven.
- Enjoy.

Amount per serving (6 total)

Timing Information:

Preparation	10 m
Cooking	1 h 15 m
Total Time	1 h 25 m

Nutritional Information:

Calories	540 kcal
Fat	32 g
Carbohydrates	9.8g
Protein	49.5 g
Cholesterol	161 mg
Sodium	699 mg

* Percent Daily Values are based on a 2,000 calorie diet.

Burgundy Beef II

Ingredients

- 1 C. beef broth
- 3 tbsps all-purpose flour
- 1 tbsp tomato paste
- 1 tsp beef demi-glace
- 3 tbsps bacon drippings
- 2 lbs beef round, cut into 3 inch pieces
- 3 tbsps sherry wine
- 1 1/2 C. chopped onions
- 1 C. Burgundy wine
- 3 sprigs fresh parsley
- 3 sprigs fresh rosemary
- 1 sprig fresh thyme
- 1 bay leaf
- 12 fresh mushrooms, sliced
- 1/4 C. butter
- 1 tbsp chopped fresh parsley, for garnish

Directions

- Get a bowl, combine: demi-glace, broth, tomato paste, and flour.
- Brown your beef in bacon drippings, then place it to the side.
- Add in the onions and the wine and cook the contents for 7 mins before adding in the tomato paste mix.
- Get everything boiling, while stirring, and add the burgundy wine.
- Grab a cheesecloth square and place in it: a bay leaf, parsley, thyme, and rosemary.
- Add this bunch of herbs to the burgundy mix.

- Place a lid on the pan and let the mix gently boil, with a low level of heat, for 3.5 hrs.
- Now stir fry your mushrooms in butter, until brown, then combine the meat with the mushrooms and cook for 17 more mins.
- Remove the herbs and add everything to a baking dish for serving.
- Top with parsley and serve.
- Enjoy.

Amount per serving (4 total)

Timing Information:

Preparation	20 m
Cooking	3 h
Total Time	3 h 20 m

Nutritional Information:

Calories	576 kcal
Fat	36.6 g
Carbohydrates	18.1g
Protein	31.8 g
Cholesterol	120 mg
Sodium	526 mg

* Percent Daily Values are based on a 2,000 calorie diet.

Buttery Egg Bites

Ingredients

- 1/4 tsp softened butter
- 2 tsps heavy cream
- 2 eggs
- salt and pepper to taste
- 1 tsp minced fresh chives
- 1 tsp grated Parmesan cheese

Directions

- Set your oven to 325 degrees before doing anything else.
- Coat your ramekins with butter and add some cream to each.
- Break the eggs over the cream and make sure the yolk of the egg is in the center of each ramekin.
- Top each one with parmesan, salt, chives, and pepper.
- Cook the contents in the oven for 14 mins then let them cool for 5 mins.
- Enjoy.

Amount per serving (1 total)

Timing Information:

Preparation	10 m
Cooking	15 m
Total Time	25 m

Nutritional Information:

Calories	196 kcal
Fat	15.2 g
Carbohydrates	1.2g
Protein	13.6 g
Cholesterol	390 mg
Sodium	1183 mg

* Percent Daily Values are based on a 2,000 calorie diet.

Crepes II

(Vegan Approved)

Ingredients

- 1/2 C. soy milk
- 1/2 C. water
- 1/4 C. melted soy margarine
- 1 tbsp turbinado sugar
- 2 tbsps maple syrup
- 1 C. unbleached all-purpose flour
- 1/4 tsp salt

Directions

- Get a bowl, combine: salt, soy milk, flour, water, syrup, 1/4 C. margarine, and sugar.
- Place a covering on the bowl and put everything in the fridge for 3 hrs.
- Coat a frying pan with margarine and then fry 3 tbsps of the mix until browned (about 3 to 4 mins). Now turn the crepe over and cook the opposite side for the same amount of time.
- Enjoy.

Amount per serving (4 total)

Timing Information:

Preparation	5 m
Cooking	20 m
Total Time	2 h 25 m

Nutritional Information:

Calories	268 kcal
Fat	12.1 g
Carbohydrates	35.6g
Protein	4.3 g
Cholesterol	0 mg
Sodium	295 mg

* Percent Daily Values are based on a 2,000 calorie diet.

Mushrooms and Angel Hair

Ingredients

- 6 skinless, boneless chicken breast halves
- 1/4 C. white wine
- salt and pepper to taste
- 1 (8 oz.) package pasta, angel hair
- 1 large white onion, chopped
- 1 tbsp chopped garlic
- 2 (8 oz.) packages sliced fresh mushrooms
- 2 C. creme fraiche
- 1/2 C. grated Parmesan cheese for topping
- 3 tbsps sour cream

Directions

- Sear your chicken in oil then add some pepper, salt, and the wine.
- Let the contents gently boil for 22 mins until the chicken is fully done.
- At the same time boil your pasta in water and salt for 9 mins. Then remove all the liquids.
- Once the chicken is done, cut it into chunks and then begin to stir fry your garlic and onions in the drippings.

- Now add the mushrooms once the onions are see-through and fry them until they become tender.
- Add in the chicken chunks, the sour cream, and the crème fraiche.
- Mix everything and get it all hot.
- Layer the creamy chicken mix over the pasta and top the contents with some parmesan.
- Enjoy.

Amount per serving (5 total)

Timing Information:

Preparation	10 m
Cooking	30 m
Total Time	1 h

Nutritional Information:

Calories	708 kcal
Fat	43.1 g
Carbohydrates	35.1g
Protein	47.6 g
Cholesterol	256 mg
Sodium	270 mg

* Percent Daily Values are based on a 2,000 calorie diet.

Apple Tenderloins

Ingredients

- 1 tbsp butter
- 1 1/2 lbs pork tenderloin
- 1 medium onion, thinly sliced
- 1 large sweet apple - peeled, cored and thinly sliced
- 1 tbsp all-purpose flour
- 5 oz. chicken stock
- 1/3 (12 fluid oz.) bottle hard apple cider
- salt and pepper to taste
- 2 tbsps heavy cream

Directions

- Set your oven to 350 degrees before doing anything else.
- Sear your pork, in butter, then place it to the side.
- Stir fry your onions for 5 mins.
- Then add the apples and fry everything for 2 more mins before adding the flour and cooking for 1 additional min.
- Get a bowl, combine: cider and stock.
- Add this to the apple mix as well as some pepper and salt.

- Add the pork back into the mix as well.
- Place a lid on the pan and place everything in the oven for 50 mins.
- Now cut your pork into thick strips.
- Puree the apple mix in a food processor then place the puree back into the pot.
- Get the mix hot again and add 2 tbsps of crème.
- Once everything is hot top your pork with this mix.
- Enjoy.

Amount per serving (6 total)

Timing Information:

Preparation	20 m
Cooking	1 h
Total Time	1 h 20 m

Nutritional Information:

Calories	204 kcal
Fat	8.4 g
Carbohydrates	9g
Protein	20.7 g
Cholesterol	72 mg
Sodium	175 mg

* Percent Daily Values are based on a 2,000 calorie diet.

Easy French Canadian Style Poutine

(Fries with Mozzarella and Gravy)

Ingredients

- 1 quart vegetable oil for frying
- 1 (10.25 oz.) can beef gravy
- 5 medium potatoes, cut into fries
- 2 C. mozzarella

Directions

- Deep fry your fries in oil while heating your gravy.
- Cook the fries for about 6 mins.
- Place the fries on some paper towel to remove the excess oils.
- Now top the fries with the cheese.
- Add the hot gravy over the cheese and let it melt from the heat.
- Enjoy hot.

Amount per serving (4 total)

Timing Information:

Preparation	5 m
Cooking	20 m
Total Time	25 m

Nutritional Information:

Calories	708 kcal
Fat	46.3 g
Carbohydrates	51g
Protein	23.8 g
Cholesterol	78 mg
Sodium	773 mg

* Percent Daily Values are based on a 2,000 calorie diet.

Mediterranean Salad

Ingredients

- 5 fresh tomatoes, cores removed, and diced
- 5 shallots, coarsely chopped
- 1/2 C. olive oil
- 1/4 C. balsamic vinegar
- 1 loaf French bread, for dipping (optional)

Directions

- Add your tomatoes to a large bowl and top them with the shallots.
- Top the mix with your balsamic and the olive oil and combine everything together.
- Let this sit for 10 mins then place a covering over the dish and put the mix in the fridge for at least 4 days.
- Serve the mix over some French bread.
- Enjoy as a dip as well.

Amount per serving (6 total)

Timing Information:

Preparation	
Cooking	10 m
Total Time	15 m

Nutritional Information:

Calories	433 kcal
Fat	19.7 g
Carbohydrates	55.3g
Protein	10.9 g
Cholesterol	0 mg
Sodium	505 mg

* Percent Daily Values are based on a 2,000 calorie diet.

Quiche II (Chards and Onions)

Ingredients

- 2 tbsps butter, divided
- 1/4 C. plain dried bread crumbs
- 2 C. 2% milk
- 8 oz. salmon fillets, skin removed
- 1/3 C. chopped onion
- 1/2 bunch Swiss chard, chopped
- 1/2 tsp salt
- 1/8 tsp ground black pepper
- 1/2 tsp dried marjoram
- 1/8 tsp ground nutmeg
- 3 eggs

Directions

- Coat a pie dish with butter and bread crumbs. Then set your oven to 350 degrees before doing anything else. Gently boil your fish in milk.
- Then place a lid on the pot and let the contents cook for 12 mins.
- Now stir fry your chards and onions, in butter, in a 2nd pot, until soft, then add: nutmeg, salt, marjoram, and pepper.
- Add the onion mix to the pie and then break up the salmon in the pie as well. Get a bowl and beat 1 C. of milk from the fish and your eggs for 1 min. Place this mix into the pie as well.
- Cook everything in the oven for 40 mins.
- Let the pie cool before serving. Enjoy.

Amount per serving (8 total)

Timing Information:

Preparation	45 m
Cooking	35 m
Total Time	1 h 20 m

Nutritional Information:

Calories	154 kcal
Fat	9.3 g
Carbohydrates	6.7g
Protein	10.8 g
Cholesterol	99 mg
Sodium	289 mg

* Percent Daily Values are based on a 2,000 calorie diet.

French Bean Casserole

Ingredients

- 2 tbsps olive oil
- 1 onion
- 2 carrots, peeled and diced
- 1 lb dry navy beans, soaked overnight
- 4 C. mushroom broth
- 1 cube vegetable bouillon
- 1 bay leaf
- 4 sprigs fresh parsley
- 1 sprig fresh rosemary
- 1 sprig fresh lemon thyme, chopped
- 1 sprig fresh savory
- 1 large potato, peeled and cubed

Directions

- With some twine, bunch together the following herbs: savory, parsley, thyme, and rosemary.
- Stir fry your carrots and onions in oil then add them to your crock pot with the following: bay leaf, beans, bouillon, and mushroom broth.
- Add some water if everything is not submerged in liquid.
- Then drop in your bunch of herbs.
- Cook the mix for 8 hrs on low and then add your potatoes and cook for 60 more mins.
- Discard the spice bunch. Enjoy.

Amount per serving (8 total)

Timing Information:

Preparation	20 m
Cooking	9 h
Total Time	9 h 20 m

Nutritional Information:

Calories	279 kcal
Fat	4.4 g
Carbohydrates	47.2g
Protein	15.3 g
Cholesterol	0 mg
Sodium	141 mg

* Percent Daily Values are based on a 2,000 calorie diet.

Salad II

(Olives, Potatoes, and Roma Tomatoes)

Ingredients

- 1/2 lb new potatoes, quartered
- 1/4 C. chopped fresh parsley
- 1/4 C. pitted nicoise olives
- 1/2 onion, thinly sliced
- 1 (6 oz.) can tuna
- 1/3 lb fresh green beans - rinsed, trimmed and blanched
- 1/2 lb mixed salad greens
- 1 C. lemon vinaigrette
- 3 hard-cooked eggs, quartered
- 3 roma (plum) tomatoes, thinly sliced
- 1 tbsp capers
- 4 anchovy filets

Directions

- Boil your potatoes in water and salt for 17 mins. Then remove all the liquid.
- Get a bowl, mix: beans, potatoes, tuna, parsley, onions, and olives.
- Place a covering on the bowl and place everything in the fridge for 5 hrs.
- Get a 2nd bowl mix: anchovies, vinaigrette, capers, tuna mix, salad greens, tomatoes, and eggs. Enjoy.

Amount per serving (4 total)

Timing Information:

Preparation	30 m
Cooking	15 m
Total Time	2 h 45 m

Nutritional Information:

Calories	299 kcal
Fat	8.8 g
Carbohydrates	34.7g
Protein	20.1 g
Cholesterol	175 mg
Sodium	1311 mg

* Percent Daily Values are based on a 2,000 calorie diet.

Quinoa XL (Creamy Casserole of Broccoli and Mushrooms)

Ingredients

- 1 C. quinoa
- 2 C. water
- 1 tsp olive oil
- 1 tsp salt
- 2 C. chopped broccoli
- 1 (10 oz.) can low-sodium cream of mushroom soup
- 1 C. shredded Cheddar cheese
- 1/2 C. French-fried onions
- 1/2 C. light sour cream
- 1 tsp lemon pepper
- salt and ground black pepper to taste
- 1/2 C. French-fried onions

Directions

- For 35 mins let your quinoa sit submerged in water.
- Then use a strainer to rinse the quinoa under cold water before boiling it in fresh water and 1 tsp of salt and olive oil.
- Once boiling place a lid on the pot, lower the heat, and let it cook for 22 mins.
- Set your oven to 350 degrees before doing anything else.

- For 7 mins steam your broccoli over 2 inches of boiling water with a steamer insert and a big pot.
- Now add the following to your quinoa: lemon pepper, broccoli, sour cream, soup, fried onions, and cheese.
- Top everything with some pepper and salt and stir everything.
- Add everything to a casserole dish and cook it all in the oven for 15 mins.
- Enjoy.

Amount per serving (6 total)

Timing Information:

Preparation	Cooking	Total Time
10 m	40 m	1 h 20 m

Nutritional Information:

Calories	494 kcal
Fat	32.1 g
Carbohydrates	39.8g
Protein	10.3 g
Cholesterol	31 mg
Sodium	1003 mg

* Percent Daily Values are based on a 2,000 calorie diet.

Thanks for Reading! Now Let's Try some Sushi and Dump Dinners....

Send the Book!

To grab this **box set** simply follow the link mentioned above, or tap the book cover.

This will take you to a page where you can simply enter your email address and a PDF version of the **box set** will be emailed to you.

I hope you are ready for some serious cooking!

Send the Book!

You will also receive updates about all my new books when they are free.

Also don't forget to like and subscribe on the social networks. I love meeting my readers. Links to all my profiles are below so please click and connect :)

Facebook

Twitter

Come On...
Let's Be Friends :)

I adore my readers and love connecting with them socially. Please follow the links below so we can connect on Facebook, Twitter, and Google+.

Facebook

Twitter

I also have a blog that I regularly update for my readers so check it out below.

My Blog

Can I Ask A Favour?

If you found this book interesting, or have otherwise found any benefit in it. Then may I ask that you post a review of it on Amazon? Nothing excites me more than new reviews, especially reviews which suggest new topics for writing. I do read all reviews and I always factor feedback into my newer works.

So if you are willing to take ten minutes to write what you sincerely thought about this book then please visit our Amazon page and post your opinions.

Again thank you!

Interested in Other Easy Cookbooks?

Everything is easy! Check out my Amazon Author page for more great cookbooks:

For a complete listing of all my books please see my author page.

Printed in France by Amazon
Brétigny-sur-Orge, FR